BETWEEN APATHY

BETWEEN APATHY AND OUTRAGE

Voluntary organisations in multiracial Britain

NAOMI CONNELLY

Policy Studies Institute

Research supported by the Joseph Rowntree Memorial Trust

PSI Publications are obtainable from all good bookshops, or by visiting the Institute at 100 Park Village East, London NW1 3SR (071-387 2171).

Sales Representation: Pinter Publishers Ltd.

Individual and Bookshop orders to: Marston Book Services Ltd, PO Box 87, Oxford, OX4 1LB.

A CIP catalogue record of this book is available from the British Library.

Research Report 700

ISBN 0 85374 463 7

Typeset by Policy Studies Institute

Printed in Great Britain by BPCC Wheaton Ltd, Exeter

Contents

Acknowledgements

This paper is based on research funded by the Joseph Rowntree Memorial Trust. I am very grateful for the Trust's support.

During the course of the research many people within the voluntary sector provided me with information, ideas and documentation. I very much appreciated their interest and co-operation. Particular thanks are due to staff of five organisations who gave especial help: Barnardo's, Contact a Family, I CAN (Invalid Children's Aid Nationwide), the National Deaf Children's Society and the Spastics Society. However, interviews were carried out in other organisations, and information was also drawn from conferences, articles and other sources. Thus when reading the paper it should not be assumed that unattributed quotations or examples are from the organisations listed above: in some cases they are, but in many others they are not.

1 Introduction

Voluntary organisations in Britain play a major role in the field of social care as providers of information, services and mutual support; as advocates and catalysts; and in many other ways. But Britain is now a multiracial society. Voluntary organisations have responded to that fact in disparate ways. Some have reacted with apathy: if they have given any thought to the matter, it has been to reject its relevance for their own work. At the other extreme, some organisations, or some people within them, have felt such a sense of outrage at the manifest inequities affecting many black people[1] in Britain that only immediate and wholesale change has been seen as acceptable. For most voluntary organisations, the approach has been somewhere in between.

There are many possible courses of action on the continuum between apathy and outrage[2] – between rejection of responsibility, and a sense of outrage so overwhelming that it can deskill and disable. An organisation may adopt a piecemeal approach, perhaps translating a leaflet into Asian languages, arranging relevant training for some staff members, announcing that it is an equal opportunities employer. Or projects designed to provide support for people from minority communities may be added somewhat precariously to an organisation's work, using special rather than mainstream funding sources, in order to meet perceived needs without a major commitment to change on the part of the organisation as a whole. Taking a different approach, an organisation may review all its operations critically and then make systematic arrangements for the changes which seem necessary.

Is it entirely up to the organisation concerned what choices are made? Or is the degree of responsibility which is accepted, and the

1

form in which this is exercised, of legitimate concern to a wider public? It can be argued that any contribution made by voluntary organisations to social care is a plus, an addition to the welfare of the country drawing on resources and experience which would not necessarily be available through statutory, commercial or not-for-profit private agencies, and we should therefore look at the positive things an organisation is doing rather than criticise it for not doing other things. Such an argument may be valid in relation to some small local voluntary groups. In most cases, however, there is legitimate public interest in what organisations do.

The Race Relations Act 1976 prohibits direct and indirect discrimination by voluntary organisations as well as by other employers and providers of services. When funds are sought from the (multiracial) public, or when grants or other forms of support come from local or central government, it is rightly a matter of concern whether these are deployed in a way which takes appropriate account of the multiracial composition of the population. When an organisation is accepted as authoritative, nationally or locally, for example in relation to a particular type of disability, and is therefore consulted about policy or about a social services department's new community care plans, or is represented on social services committee, community health council or other body, it is important to know whether the interests of all those with the particular disability are adequately understood. The same is true when a voluntary body is a major, or even sole, provider of a particular kind of service, or of services to particular groups of people. Section 9 of the Disabled Persons (Services, Consultation and Representation) Act 1986 requires social services departments to ensure that information about relevant services from both statutory and voluntary sources is made available to disabled people; those preparing and using lists or guides need to be confident that voluntary agencies included are equipped to meet the needs of people from diverse communities.

Most important of all, when individual black people are in need of information, advice, support or care, they should – as a matter of social justice – have equal access to sources of these, whether that access is through voluntary organisations or statutory agencies.

The voluntary sector includes a substantial number of black self-help groups and black-managed organisations.[3] Many of these have been established to meet needs which have been ignored, or met inadequately, by statutory agencies or the predominantly-white voluntary sector. In some circumstances, a black person may prefer to approach a black organisation, if a relevant one is available. However, the term 'black', while useful shorthand, covers a tremendous diversity of countries of origin, religions, languages and customs. It cannot be assumed that because an organisation exists it will be the appropriate one for a particular individual or group, or will be the preferred option. Even if it is both appropriate and preferred, the organisation may not be able to take on additional tasks: black organisations are frequently overstretched and underresourced.[4] Thus, although the presence or absence of black voluntary organisations is a matter of some importance to predominantly-white national and local voluntary groups, the importance lies in finding the right relationship. Issues about such relationships need to be on the agenda when organisations review their roles and responsibilities: the existence of relevant black organisations does not mean that review is unnecessary.

The changing context

Like all providers of support and care, the voluntary sector is going through a period of change. A major question is the extent to which, over the next few years, voluntary organisations will be taking on responsibilities for services currently provided by social services departments, and whether this will be financed through existing types of funding relationships, through winning contracts put out to competitive tender, or in other ways. The challenges presented come as an addition to many other challenges affecting the voluntary sector or some parts of it in recent years. The movement away from provision of residential services to a variety of day facilities and domiciliary support arrangements has been a significant one for a number of well-established service-providing organisations. In some cases this has gone along with a movement towards working with families and with local community groups, rather than with children or adults in a more isolated way. The growth of self-help and user groups among those with particular diseases or disabilities, and the development of disabled people's organisations locally and nationally, have spurred substantial rethinking in some traditional organisations.

A rather different challenge has come as some service-providing voluntary organisations have found themselves in competition for users with an expanding commercial sector of care. The growth of this sector during the 1980s, especially in residential care, is attributable in large part to the availability of social security benefits. Changes in benefit arrangements in 1988 (and especially the introduction of the Social Fund) raised new questions for voluntary organisations about the kinds of support they could and should make available to individuals in need. Another central government policy which has had a major impact on the voluntary sector has been the Manpower Services Commission's Community Programme. Many organisations expanded their operations very substantially in the mid-1980s to take advantage of this – and then found it necessary to retrench following the 1988 change to Employment Training.

Some organisations have thus far been affected only marginally by these developments; some have been drastically affected by many of them. But it is a time for rethinking throughout the voluntary sector.

Race equality on the agenda

In this period of challenging change, how do voluntary organisations view the additional challenge of finding an appropriate role in a multiracial, multicultural society? To what extent do issues of race equality routinely form part of discussions about the functioning of individual organisations? In recent years there has been a major growth of interest in issues of race equality in the voluntary sector. The subject has been increasingly discussed within organisations, and in working parties, conferences and workshops which have provided a forum for exchange of information among voluntary organisations or between statutory and voluntary agencies. In some cases concern has focussed on anti-racism or on race equality, while in others wider equal opportunity issues have been addressed. Some discussion has related specifically to employment while some has covered all aspects of the functioning of organisations, from composition of management committees to the support and care provided to members or service users.

Publications which present the issues and suggest ways of proceeding have increasingly become available. The 1984 report of the NCVO Ethnic Minorities Working Party, *A Multi-Racial Society: The role of national voluntary organisations,*[5] has been followed by guidance from the Volunteer Centre,[6] British Association of Settlements and Social Action Centres,[7] London Voluntary Service

Council,[8] North Kensington Law Centre,[9] MIND South East,[10] Councils of Voluntary Service National Association[11] and others.[12]

These publications are intended to encourage change, and to give guidance as to how change can be achieved. This paper has the same starting points: a commitment to race equality, and a view that voluntary organisations, like statutory agencies, have a responsibility to take account of the multiracial, multicultural nature of British society. The aim of this paper, however, is not to give specific guidance, but rather to explore how roles and responsibilities are defined, and the steps which are being taken within some organisations. The process of change has been slow and uneven in the voluntary sector as in local authorities and other agencies: if more can be learned about this process, it may be possible to move more quickly and effectively towards race equality.[13]

Material for the paper was drawn from a variety of sources. The most important were formal interviews and informal discussions during 1986 and 1987 with staff of a number of national voluntary organisations, with people working in cross-organisation development posts, and with others (inside and outside the voluntary sector) having specific interest and expertise in the issues being explored. As a way into 'the voluntary sector' the study focussed initially on national organisations whose concern in part or primarily was people with physical disabilities, although as much information as possible was collected about what was happening elsewhere in the voluntary sector.

Except for the material available in the NCVO 1984 Working Party report, little information was available at the time the project began about how the issues were being defined and what steps were being taken and why. The study was therefore planned as an exploratory one among organisations which had already taken at least one initiative indicating recognition that change might be necessary. Interviews were held with senior officers of ten national organisations: these revealed a wide range of attitudes and levels of activity, and further work was concentrated on those organisations in which substantial activity seemed to be taking place at headquarters or local levels. Since the research was completed there have been numerous changes in these and other national voluntary organisations.

Although some of the findings relate specifically to organisations concerned with disability, most of the issues which arose during the research have much wider relevance. The paper has therefore been written largely in terms of 'voluntary organisations', and its subtitle reflects this.

Plan of the paper

Just as a wide range of views about responsibilities in a multiracial society can be found across the voluntary sector, within any individual organisation there will be a variety of viewpoints about what an appropriate role might be and why. The views of directors and other senior staff are likely to be of particular importance in understanding the potential for change in the direction of race equality, and chapter two examines the ideas expressed – some of which seem likely to inhibit systematic development of policies towards race equality, while others provide a spur to change.

Although some of the views held, some aspects of the functioning of organisations and some of the pressures coming from outside organisations imply taking a particular step or filling a specific gap, for the most part an organisation which accepts the need for change has many choices both about what to do and how to do it. Chapter three looks at some aspects of the work of voluntary organisations where change has been taking place. Examples are given of the kinds of activities undertaken, whether these are piecemeal, precarious or planned.

Consideration of the varied attitudes and the varied ways of tackling change provokes a number of questions about roles, responsibilities and the practicalities of introducing change. These questions are explored in chapter four, drawing on the experience of organisations at various stages of development of policy and practice. A final chapter provides a summary and goes on to draw attention to possible implications of the new relationships among providers of social care.

Notes

1   In any discussion of race equality, terminology presents a problem. While focussing attention on the language of 'race' can aid sensitive use of words, clear thinking and improved communication of ideas and experience, a possible disadvantage is if much-needed discussion is inhibited because of anxiety about using incorrect, inappropriate or offensive language. In this paper, 'black people' is used to refer to people of African, Asian or Caribbean origins. Like all the other words and phrases we have available, the phrase is one of a number of possible ways of referring to a diverse and complex reality.

It has both advantages and limitations, and is accepted by some people and not others; however, some words have to be chosen if issues are to be discussed.

2   I am indebted to Gordon Peters, Director of Social Services, London Borough of Hackney, for the phrase 'between apathy and outrage', which he used at a 1987 Study Day on 'Implications of the Transcultural Model of Social Work Education and Training'. He was referring to the range of attitudes in a social services department, but the phrase seemed to me especially appropriate when applied to the voluntary sector.

3   The black and ethnic minority voluntary sector is particularly well developed in London. See Pascoe Sawyers and Joy Fraser, *Bridges: A Directory of African, Caribbean, Asian, Latin American and Mediterranean Community Groups in Greater London*, London Voluntary Service Council, 1988.

4   Maureen Stone, *Resourcing Black Voluntary Organisations: Funding for failure?*, Report to the NCVO Urban Unit, 1986; and Barry Knight and Anne Marie McDonald, *The Funding Relationship: Report of a conference on the funding of organisations managed by members of ethnic minorities*, Home Office Voluntary Services Unit, 1988.

5   Michaela Dungate, *A Multi-Racial Society: The role of national voluntary organisations*, NCVO, 1984.

6   See, for example, Pradeep Kumar, *Ethnic Monitoring and VBX*, Berkhamsted, Volunteer Centre, 1986.

7   Paul Davison, *Ideas into Action: Notes produced by a BASSAC members' workshop*, British Association of Settlements and Social Action Centres, 1986.

8   Christine Collins, 'We want to be anti-racist but we don't know what to do', London Voluntary Service Council, 1986. One case study included is that of Southwark Council for Voluntary Service, which in 1984 published its own booklet on *Equal Opportunities: Some steps towards race equality in employment*.

9   Kate Poulton, *Equal Opportunity Employment Policies: Guidelines for voluntary organisations*, North Kensington Law Centre Employment Rights Unit, 1986.

10 Sheena Dunbar and Laurence Ward, *A Guide to the Implementation of an Equal Opportunity Policy*, MIND South East, 1987.

11 Priscilla Annamanthodo, *Racism in Britain: Guidance for CVS and other local development agencies*, CVS-NA, 1987 and Coreen Allen and Judy Walker, *Implementing an Equal Opportunities Policy: A guideline for CVS*, CVS-NA, 1987.

12 For example, Jim Read, *The Equal Opportunities Book: A guide to employment practice in voluntary organisations and community groups*,

InterChange Books, 1988. The Scottish Council for Voluntary Organisations have produced a report on their race equality action-research project: Lucy Macleod, *"Irrespective of race, colour or creed?": Voluntary organisations and minority ethnic groups in Scotland*, SCVO, 1987. An account of Brighton CVS's race equality project is given by Marc Jaffrey and Alan Farleigh in *Action not Words: Putting a race equality policy into practice*, Brighton CVS, 1988.

13 For discussion of the process of change in social services departments, see Naomi Connelly, *Race and Change in Social Services Departments*, PSI, 1989.

2 Roles and responsibilities

A wide range of views about appropriate roles and responsibilities in a multiracial society can be found across the voluntary sector as a whole, but also often within an individual voluntary organisation. That is certain to be so in organisations with hundreds of employees. Even in small organisations, once the unspoken understandings are breached and race equality issues are discussed specifically, there may well be different viewpoints about the priority to be given to the subject and the form any changes should take.

The more complex the organisation, the more scope there is for such diversity. Paid employees at headquarters and in the field, voluntary members of management and executive committees, voluntary fundraisers or service providers, local branch or group members and regular service users all may have different conceptions of the role and responsibilities of the organisation. Within each of these categories there will be a range of views as well. Yet in organisations whose concern is information, advice, support or care for vulnerable people, a considerable degree of consensus is probably necessary if effective change towards race equality is to occur.

That has certainly been the experience in social services departments, but consensus may be even more necessary in the voluntary sector. When people are contributing their time on a voluntary basis, whether as members of management committees, as fundraisers, as branch officers or in other ways, they need not continue if they are not in accord with the decisions taken. Paid workers may have chosen to work in the voluntary sector, or in a particular voluntary organisation, because of what they see as its special ethos; in some cases their need to be convinced of the rightness of any particular course adopted may be even greater than would be the case in the statutory sector. Given the chronic shortage of funds in most voluntary organisations, and the efforts required to obtain sufficient funding from a variety of sources, there may be particular hurdles to overcome when suggestions are made for using resources to support activities related to introduction of race equality or equal opportunity programmes.

The role of senior staff

In attempting to understand the potential for change towards race equality in a voluntary organisation, it is therefore important to understand the range of views. All are important, but those of directors and other senior staff can be crucial for influencing the way in which an organisation approaches the possibility of change, and the amount of change which gets underway. In recent years some directors have been appointed with a remit to change the organisation, and in a few cases this remit has explicitly included helping the organisation adapt to a multiracial society. Even in such cases, there is likely to be a variety of views within the organisation about tactics, and about the degree of priority to be accorded to race equality policies when weighed against either traditional activities or other new developments (including other aspects of equal opportunities).

Directors and other senior staff can encourage initiatives, or at least not block them. They can introduce ideas to management committees, whose members may have specialist medical, financial or other expertise, but be unaware of changing equal opportunity developments within the statutory and voluntary sectors. They may be able to introduce ideas to branch members, user groups, parents or others, to whom it has not necessarily occurred that the organisation might have wider responsibilities than those currently undertaken. Once change is underway, directors and other senior staff can influence the extent to which implementation of specific initiatives proves successful, and the extent to which there is change in the culture of the organisation, by ensuring adequate training and other resources are available, providing backing to staff when difficulties arise, and in other ways.

Personalities, tactical and political adeptness, organisational structures and the ethos of the organisation can all affect the degree of influence any particular senior officer is able to exert. The diversity and complexity of national voluntary organisations mean that a wide range of both attitudes and activity are likely within a particular organisation at any one time, and doubtless in all organisations there are changes taking place at local levels which do not come to the attention of headquarters staff. Nevertheless, knowledge of the views of senior staff can be helpful in understanding the potential for change, and the potential for systematic change.

Certainties and uncertainties

Considerable diversity of opinion was found during the interviewing carried out for this project. The views of the senior officers interviewed could be placed roughly on a continuum of awareness or interest in issues of race equality – a continuum ranging from apparent unease or distaste for change through to whole-hearted commitment to race equality and the changes necessary to bring this about. What was striking, however, was not just that there were differences between those in different organisations, but also that there seemed to be many strands within the ideas expressed by individuals. Perhaps most frequently found was a complex mix of sentiments, and uncertainty (sometimes explicitly voiced) about appropriate steps for the organisation.

Some of the views expressed seemed likely to act as a constraint on systematic consideration of the organisation's role in a multiracial society, although they would not necessarily inhibit the adoption of piecemeal steps advocated or initiated by others in the organisation. On the other hand, some of the views appeared to provide a constructive force for change – in some cases, systematic and thoroughgoing change.

None of those interviewed was 'colourblind' in the sense found by Juliet Cheetham in social services departments ten years ago:[1]

> Some respondents said they did not know which of their clients were black. They were then asked if they knew which were men and women, a question which some thought silly. It was asked deliberately to estimate the strength of the principle of non-categorisation.

She goes on to say:

> When social workers maintain that they are ignorant of their client's colour it is almost certainly a well-meaning self deception, meant to imply that colour and ethnicity are not the most important facts about an individual, and will not entail discriminatory

> treatment ... Most social workers would regard culture, education and class as significant in ... assessment. They find it harder to include ethnicity, perhaps largely because of fears that differences associated with race or colour will be perceived negatively.

As the organisations contacted for this project were those known to have taken at least one step which indicated an awareness that they were working in a multiracial, multicultural society, it is perhaps not unexpected that 'colourblindness' of this kind was not found among senior staff. But it may also be due to a changed climate of discussion about race equality issues in the social care world, which is likely to have affected London headquarters officers of national organisations even if not all staff, volunteers, local group members or management committee members.

However, 'colourblind' still seems the most useful description for a complex of attitudes, among which it is possible to distinguish some aspects which were negative, some which could be characterised as passive, and some as active. Thus, one director outlined a number of activities which had been undertaken in his organisation, saying that 'naturally' the needs of a more diverse population would be taken into account. At the same time he showed some resentment at the situation, commenting in an aside 'they really ought to learn English'; he summed up his view by saying 'A pity to draw it out and make an issue of it. It becomes a political issue.'[2]

More common was a passive colourblindness, where those interviewed appeared to have given little thought to whether any steps were necessary to take account of Britain's multiracial populations – or at least any steps beyond the kind of routine acknowledgement represented by translation of a leaflet or, as one director said, 'Of course we put "equal opportunity employer" in advertisements'. From such viewpoints, nothing was stopping black people from joining the organisation or making use of its services. Indeed, it was pointed out in a number of cases that some branches were known to have Afro-Caribbean or Asian members, or it was noted that there was no reason why headquarters should be aware of whether there were such members in local groups or not.

Sometimes there was a more active emphasis on colourblindness, and it was clearly a point of pride to be able to say, as one director did, 'Colour makes no difference to the service we provide'. The basis of this may be a strongly-held ethos about service to individuals (as Juliet

Cheetham suggests), so that it is not really that 'colour makes no difference' but rather that no barriers will be erected to keep out individual black people, no discrimination will take place on grounds of colour, and any special factors relating to culture/race/religion are expected to be taken into account routinely in dealing with an individual.

When senior staff show greater explicit concern than this with diversity they do not necessarily see specific implications for the work of their own organisation, or they may be ambivalent or reluctant about making deliberate changes. This may be because of the nature of the particular organisation, the kinds of people working in it or the people it serves.

Where organisations have been established specifically as membership organisations of those with a particular disability, this has often been in reaction against traditional service-providing organisations. In such cases, it is an important part of the ethos of the organisation that members make the decisions. One such organisation was therefore described as awaiting black members, or awaiting specific suggestions from any existing black members. If they made their voice heard about changes necessary, senior staff would take this on board: until then, little could be done. In another organisation, the director argued that having the particular disability overrode all other considerations, and it would therefore be wrong to differentiate among those with the disability.

When race equality is accepted as relevant to the organisation, senior staff sometimes argue that there is no need to take any specific steps, or any beyond the bare minimum: their view is that the organisation is equipped to make the necessary adjustments as the need arises. Sometimes this is ascribed to professionalism, and in one organisation headquarters staff were confident that their field staff (described as 'very professional, very skilled in assessing needs') would themselves take any steps which they felt were necessary to improve their practice in multiracial areas: 'We truly have not had difficulties'. At headquarters, no equal opportunities programme was thought to be required as 'senior management's view is self-evident'.

In other cases, the lack of need to take specific steps is ascribed to the sort of people staffing the organisation: they would automatically do the right thing. Thus, one director said that senior staff were 'easy and relaxed about it' although he then added 'We've carried on happily

13

not discriminating and have therefore perhaps not noticed when we *are* discriminating'. Another director referred to the 'inherent decency' of his senior staff: their social work or community work backgrounds, and their experience of work among people with disabilities, meant that they had always had an awareness of equal opportunity issues together with the necessary sensitivity and empathy. In this organisation, a deliberate decision had been taken not to have a full-scale equal opportunity programme, but instead to rely on 'the vigilance and consciousness of senior staff' – although recognising that this might prove inadequate, given the many sites and large numbers of staff involved.

One director was confident that her organisation could routinely make any necessary adjustments in support to a more diverse membership, but felt that she had a responsibility to draw issues relating to the particular disability to the attention of statutory service providers: 'It's a professional challenge, nothing to do with us'. If people with disabilities were not getting equal access to public services, they were not getting a fair deal, and there was therefore a responsibility for her and others like her to do something about it; she described this as 'an old-fashioned way of being British'.

Yet another strand in thinking was represented by the director who pointed out that where his organisation provided services in multiracial areas, black people were already using them. He and his colleagues could see the need to take more specific steps where the people involved were Asians with limited command of English, living in very deprived circumstances, and with very different cultures: indeed, in some parts of the country projects were being established to meet their needs. However, he argued that it would be patronising and dependency-creating to take steps specifically to provide support for Afro-Caribbeans, who were quite competent to take the initiative and make an approach if they needed something different from what was currently available.

Spurs to change
Both the certainties and uncertainties expressed by senior staff often seemed very personal responses to the question of the role and responsibilities of their organisations. In many cases, however, specific spurs to change were identified – whether from inside or outside the organisation.

Sometimes the overall ethos of the organisation gives a lead. Thus, for example, David Cheeseman, chief officer of Councils of Voluntary Service-National Association, has written:

> It became apparent to CVSNA that combating racism and working for a better deal for black people was not just a current issue but part of its philosophy of justice and equality of opportunity for all.[3]

Reliance on particular aspects of an organisation's ethos can, of course, in some cases encourage complacency; on the other hand, in some circumstances the value placed, say, on professionalism or internationalism can provide a necessary spur to change, at least insofar as it encourages greater awareness of diversity, and consideration of ways of meeting this. Thus, one director stressed that it was a point of professional pride that no one with the disability concerned had ever been turned away by the organisation, however difficult the case. In another organisation a policy officer described his view of professionalism as implying *really* meeting changing needs.

Many disability organisations have international links, and in a few cases translations of information about the disability had originally been planned or carried out to meet the needs of those abroad, and only then had it been realised that they could be useful in Britain itself. One organisation with premises in central London pointed to its role in meeting enquiries about disability from overseas visitors (largely from the middle east) staying at nearby hotels.

Religious affiliation can present some difficulties but also some incentive to rethink the implications of an organisation's ethos. In one organisation, when children had been cared for in residential settings it had seemed clear that the framework for this should be specifically Christian commitment and teaching. Now that the work carried out was largely in the community, and with families of many different persuasions, one officer argued that the Christian ethos of the organisation could continue to be expressed, but as 'a sense of justice', 'a desire to be inclusive rather than exclusive' and 'concern for the underprivileged'.

Although, as noted above, an organisation's concern with disability can sometimes inhibit the tackling of race equality issues, the opposite was also found. Some of the points made by those interviewed were about sensitivity in relation to other issues of oppression or discrimination that came from having a disability and/or working in an organisation with people who might also suffer oppression. One officer noted that 'it seemed natural to us to work on equal opportunities', including issues relating to race equality; another had drawn explicitly on arguments currently being used in relation to race equality in arguing for consultation with and self-determination for people with disabilities. In one case, a breakthrough in committee members' understanding was said to have come when skilled external trainers drew effective parallels between the experience of those with the disability which was the concern of the organisation, and the experience of black people.

Constraints on change

Senior staff in some cases made plain their personal view that their organisation needed to make changes if it was to function adequately in a multiracial society, but they then drew attention to the constraints impeding this. Lack of support (or active opposition) in some part of the organisation was frequently mentioned. As noted earlier, in any organisation there is likely to be a range of views. Sometimes management and executive committees are unenthusiastic, and make it difficult or impossible for staff to take positive steps in the direction of race equality. Jean Ellis has highlighted some of the issues in her discussion of 'Management committees and race equality', with illustrative case studies of three organisations 'within the broad sphere of community/social work and/or advice giving'.[4] In the case of national organisations, committee members are often chosen from among 'the great and the good' – people who may have little time to spare to discuss what they view as issues extraneous to the contribution they expect to make through professional or financial advice.

Members of local branches, or active local volunteers, are sometimes said to have difficulty understanding or accepting positive steps towards race equality taken by headquarters.[5] In one self-help organisation local branches were questioning the appointment of workers specifically to develop support for black people as they saw this as a reflection on the quality of their own openness to black members, and in any case felt that if there were resources available for development existing members and groups should have priority. Staff, too, may be resistant, and in another organisation introduction of an equal opportunity employment programme had been put aside at least temporarily because of opposition from disabled staff: as they had obtained their posts without such a programme, they were reported to argue that others should do the same.

On the other hand, in some organisations questions of race equality, or of services to ethnic minority communities, had been raised forcefully by members of management or other committees, by concerned members of multiracial local groups or branches, or by staff coming in from local authorities or voluntary agencies which had already embarked on change. In this context, one officer pointed to the importance for his organisation of having structures which allowed staff at all levels to say things – and to be heard – despite the organisation's size and its many areas of work. Directors who had a personal commitment to moving the organisation on were clearly both heartened and strengthened when initiatives and support were forthcoming from across many levels of the organisation.

But even when there is consensus about the need to do something, given the now multiracial composition of the population, or the population served by the organisation, a significant constraint on effective change is sometimes uncertainty about the right thing to do, and anxiety about doing the wrong thing. The uncertainty is captured in the title of Christine Collins' 1986 collection of case studies for the London Voluntary Service Council: *'We want to be anti-racist but we don't know what to do'*. The anxiety is captured in the somewhat embarrassed explanation of an experienced voluntary sector worker that 'we freeze' when confronted with issues of race, because of worry about putting a foot wrong; she added grimly that this did not seem to be an inhibiting factor in anything else they did.[6]

There is a danger that this combination of uncertainty and anxiety, coupled with an overwhelming sense of outrage, can sometimes deskill and disable: Priscilla Annamanthodo, in urging clear objectives, has referred to the danger of 'a murky ill-defined mass of "anti-racism"'.[7] The question of what goals organisations of particular kinds can appropriately set is raised by consideration of statements such as the following, from Southwark Council for Voluntary Service:

> SCVS accepts that if it is to be acknowledged as an anti racist agency, it must have an understanding of the broader issues affecting Black people in Britain and elsewhere, and to take a stand on such issues as anti-apartheid, policing, third world development.[8]

Even more thought-provoking is Jean Ellis' argument that:

> Anti-racism has such wide-reaching ramifications that it can be
> successfully tackled only by questioning every held assumption
> about what to do and how to do it.[9]

There are a few national organisations which have had no need to
go through soul-searching of the kind so often apparent in voluntary
organisations. Some have been formed relatively recently, with an
awareness of the need to take account of issues arising in multiracial
areas. There are still decisions to be made take about how explicit work
directed towards race equality needs to be and how high a profile such
work should take, but making such decisions is easier because staff
and management committees start from a common basis. The issues
to be tackled can then be defined differently: not whether the
organisation can take responsibility, nor why those involved should
do so – but what they should do and how to do it most effectively.
Even so, national organisations are too complex for change of any kind
to be an easy matter, and change in the direction of race equality itself
is inevitably complex.

The many interrelated strands of thinking set out above are
important: they provide the context within which issues are defined,
opportunities taken, responsibilities accepted. But many other factors,
inside and outside the organisation, have an impact on what change is
introduced, in what way, and how effectively. Chapter three looks at
some of these factors, and at the kind of steps being taken by
organisations.

Notes

1   Juliet Cheetham, *Social Work Services for Ethnic Minorities in Britain and
    the U.S.A.: Final report of a study funded by the Department of Health and
    Social Security*, University of Oxford Department of Social and
    Administrative Studies, 1981, p.26.

2   The Charity Commission's 1983 report clarified the question of whether 'the
    promotion of good race relations' was political or charitable: 'We took the
    view that the promotion of racial harmony or good race relations is analogous
    to purposes which the Courts have held to be charitable ... We agreed ... that
    promoting good race relations, endeavouring to eliminate discrimination on
    grounds of race and encouraging equality of opportunity between persons of
    different racial groups were charitable purposes.' Reprinted in Charity
    Commissioners for England and Wales, *The Promotion of Racial Harmony*,
    booklet CC17, 1989.

3   David Cheeseman, p.x of the Foreword to Priscilla Annamanthodo's *Racism in Britain*, CVS-NA, 1987.

4   Jean Ellis, 'Management committees and race equality: anti-racism in the voluntary sector – a picture of inaction', Supplement to NCVO *MDU Bulletin*, no.5, June 1985.

5   Judith Citron has explored issues of headquarters-local office communication gaps (including those concerning equal opportunities) in her study of *Citizens Advice Bureaux: For the community, by the community*, Pluto Press, 1989; see especially pp.144-147, 'Signs of the communications gap'. Ann Richardson and Meg Goodman have drawn attention to the fact that 'Self-help groups are, whatever their affiliation, essentially local bodies. Their members are naturally concerned primarily with their own needs ... it is important to recognise the essentially limited horizons of their own effective worlds' (*Self-Help and Social Care*, Policy Studies Institute, 1983, p.52).

6   David N. Thomas discusses communication difficulties between black people and white people, and the factors which seem to be inhibiting white community workers, in *White Bolts, Black Locks: Participation in the inner city*, Allen & Unwin, 1986.

7   Priscilla Annamanthodo, *Racism in Britain: Guidance for CVS and other local development agencies*, CVS-NA, 1987, p.62.

8   Southwark Council for Voluntary Service, quoted in Christine Collins, '*We want to be anti-racist but we don't know what to do*', London Voluntary Service Council, 1986, p.12.

9   Jean Ellis, 'Management committees and race equality: anti-racism in the voluntary sector – a picture of inaction', Supplement to NCVO *MDU Bulletin*, no.5, June 1985.

3 Change: piecemeal, precarious or planned

Although the ethos of the organisation and the attitudes and experience of senior staff and others are important, many factors affect the way in which organisations define their roles and responsibilities in a multiracial society. Some of these imply a specific course of action, for example when a glaring gap in the organisation's functioning is identified, or pressure is applied by a local authority with which joint working is planned, or resources become available for particular types of activity. In other cases – probably the majority – there are many choices available about what the scope and content of change should be.

Not only is there a vast range of possibilities from which to choose, but also there are a variety of methods of tackling the matter: change can be piecemeal, precarious or planned. Almost any activity can be one or the other. Even the apparently simple step of translation of a leaflet – so often the first step taken by a voluntary organisation – can be an isolated initiative; or the decision can hinge precariously on the availability of special funding; or production of the translation can be part of a wider and carefully planned programme of change.

There are advantages and disadvantages in each of these methods. Piecemeal or precarious steps are frequently ad hoc or intended merely as tokens, but they may also be devised as pilots for further more systematic change. They may represent the maximum which the organisation as a whole wants to do at any particular time, or they may seem to committed staff the most substantial steps possible when there is lack of enthusiasm for adaptation at critical points in the organisation. Piecemeal and precarious steps may meet few of the intended aims because they are carried out with insufficient knowledge or experience or support, or they may make a critical difference to those black people reached. Careful planning can ensure that some pitfalls are avoided, and that necessary change begins to take place, but the number of unknowns is always so great, and the organisational implications often so substantial, that even with careful planning there may be obstacles and setbacks. Thus, a considerable degree of commitment and flexibility is required whichever approach is adopted.

By now, the starting point for headquarters of national organisations is less likely than a few years ago to be a blank sheet. Race equality issues have a much higher profile throughout the social care world, and are increasingly discussed at conferences, workshops and in training courses. The social services press carries frequent articles about current issues of concern and about particular projects, of relevance to those in the voluntary sector as well as in social services departments. Both central and local government have shown increasing interest in the extent to which funded voluntary organisations recognise the equal opportunity aspects of their work. Where black populations are substantial, local members or groups, and project and development staff, are likely to have had their awareness raised and may well have made incremental adjustments to their ways of working by the time issues are considered at headquarters.

The guides for voluntary organisations listed in chapter one make clear the many areas of operation which a complex national organisation needs to tackle. These include consultation with black groups, ensuring as full involvement as possible of black people in all levels of the work of the organisation, changed recruitment and selection procedures for both paid staff and volunteers, examination of the relevance and quality of services offered, and many others. Little information is yet available about how much of this agenda has been tackled in individual organisations, the problems which have been met and how these have been overcome.

People in development roles commonly report difficulty in getting organisations to share their detailed experience openly. However great the degree of commitment to change, the tentative steps taken in many voluntary groups during the 1980s have often been fraught with dissension, have exposed inadequacies in general organisational arrangements, and have raised disconcerting questions about how much common understanding and consensus there actually is in the organisation. Yet it is likely that in voluntary organisations as in social services departments it is those people who have tried hardest to implement change who are most dissatisfied with their efforts and most aware of how much is still to be accomplished. Whatever the inadequacies they see in what they have achieved, their experience doubtless has much to teach other organisations.[1]

The exploratory study which is the basis of this paper was not intended to provide detailed case studies of individual organisations but the information collected gives some picture of the variety of ways in which organisations tackle particular areas of operation. Among these are getting an information base, opening up the organisation to a wider group of people, and raising awareness in the organisation. All these overlap and are interrelated, but they are addressed separately below for ease of discussion.

Getting an information base
One director commented that need was responded to 'as, when and where it manifests itself'. Such an ad hoc approach has been the traditional one, in social services departments as in the voluntary sector. Despite the increase in policy-level interest in issues of race equality both in the statutory and voluntary sectors, this is probably still the most common approach. But as organisations have begun to consider the possibility of change in what they provide and how they operate, they have begun to look more systematically at what needs there might be, rather than tackling them solely on a case-by-case basis.

However, 'need' can be defined in many different ways, and how it is defined influences both the information sought and the methods adopted to obtain it. Information can be sought about the characteristics and circumstances of black populations, locally and nationally, and about the implications of these for possible need for the services provided by the organisation. The 'need' may appear to be for information about what other organisations or agencies are providing (locally, regionally or nationally) and what gaps appear to them to need filling. The starting point for information collection can be the organisation itself: the extent to which black people are currently involved and their satisfaction with this, the levels of awareness and knowledge among existing staff, and so on. Or the priority 'need' may be for information about how organisational change has been implemented elsewhere and which aspects of the experience gained can be drawn on.

The methods of getting an information base are equally varied, and range from tapping the views of a few statutory service-providers to large-scale surveys and service reviews, from informal discussion with a few black informants to formal consultation exercises, from reliance on the spin-offs of having a few black staff to working parties and other structures for considering policies and practices.

Sometimes an information collection exercise is the first step, or one of a number of continuing steps, in a programme of work specifically on race equality; sometimes information about black people is sought as one aspect of the routine information collection arrangements of the organisation. Sometimes the initiative is taken by one region or one local officer, sometimes by headquarters. Sometimes 'need' is seen largely in terms of lack of knowledge of services, little command of English, and isolation because of cultural or other factors, combined with the complex of inner city problems; sometimes it is defined (instead or in addition) in terms of experience of discrimination and racism, with their effects on access to services and equal treatment within them.

An early (and comprehensive) survey was Barnardo's 1966 *Racial Integration and Barnardo's: Report of a working party*. The working party's terms of reference were 'To report on the position with regard to children of non-European descent in Dr.Barnardo's, whether in residential care or otherwise; to examine the problems arising, and to make recommendations': the annual return showing 'proportion of coloured children below school-leaving age' in the care of the organisation had shown a rise from 15 per cent in 1961 to 20 per cent in 1965, with the increase much more marked in some areas than others. The working party took evidence from staff, statutory agencies and voluntary agencies on issues concerning residential care, adoption and fostering, and aftercare; and evidence from 25 young 'coloured' people (aged 14-26) who were or had been in the organisation's care, about their 'colour consciousness', their experience of prejudice, and their suggestions for changes in Barnardo's functioning.

A more recent example from Barnardo's is the London Division's 1984 examination of the views of Newham residents of a variety of ethnic origins, and the views of local service providers, about the needs of children and their families;[2] the survey was carried out as a basis for planning new projects in the London borough. In the North West, the Spastics Society regional officer undertook research in 1977 among local community relations officers and a welfare association in order to ascertain any additional problems faced by Asian families with a handicapped member; following the study, an Asian community worker was appointed to begin to meet some of the needs found, but funding was made available for only a brief period. In the West Midlands, ICAN's regional officer and an Asian research worker produced a report in 1985 on the views of 23 families in Smethwick with handicapped children.[3] Practical problems which became apparent during the course of the interviewing were referred to relevant agencies, and the report was followed by the establishment of a number of projects funded through the Community Programme and Opportunities for Volunteering.

Consultation to ascertain need is sometimes fairly ad hoc, sometimes carefully planned. Staff of voluntary organisations concerned with health and welfare place great importance on their relationship with health and social services staff. The views of such staff (whether social services directors, area office managers, health visitors or others) are often sought before projects are planned. The aim is partly defensive, so that the voluntary organisation will not appear to be poaching on statutory territory; partly ground-laying for effective cross-referral when projects get off the ground; and partly to obtain information about need.

In some cases, the initiative is taken by local health authority, social services or education department staff rather than the voluntary organisation. A number of regional or local officers spoke of having been pressed for some years to meet needs which staff of the statutory agencies saw clearly but felt that they themselves were (for resource or other reasons) unable to meet. One organisation, responding to such pressure, had put off consultation with local black groups as it seemed more important to get a project off the ground so there would be something specific to consult about. The project was deliberately intended to be as flexible as possible, so that the gradual learning which was expected about needs and how to meet them could be incorporated into the project's functioning. It was hoped that in this way it would be possible to avoid some of the problems faced elsewhere when 'need' was defined by statutory service providers, and existing resources or methods of coping within local black communities were underestimated or misunderstood.

A different approach towards consultation was adopted by the National Deaf Children's Society (NDCS), whose Education Officer raised issues about hearing impairment and disability, and the possible needs of black families, with a range of black organisations. This was followed by an open 'advisory meeting' for black families in 1985, at which they discussed the ways in which the organisation might change; the meeting was reported in the Society's journal, *Talk*, along with interviews with black parents and articles about the professional and educational issues involved.[4]

When organisations have a general idea of what needs might be, but are uncertain about the exact content of relevant change, they sometimes make a specialist appointment of a community or social worker, and hope that needs of individuals will be uncovered and met. Depending on the person who is appointed, and the openness of the organisation to learning, the appointment can sometimes prove a major source of information not just about unmet need among existing service users and others in local black communities, but about the aims and practicalities of change in the organisation. In one organisation, supervision sessions with a specialist development worker were clearly seen as a two-way learning process by the senior staff member involved; individual members of staff were said to be spending days working alongside the development worker to learn from her; and she was contributing ideas and experience at other points within the organisation, local statutory agencies and the voluntary sector.

As with specialist staff in social services departments, voluntary organisations sometimes find they need to protect their staff from the demands for information (or interpreting) by other voluntary and statutory agencies; or from their own overloading and over-expectations of what one person can provide. Some of these latter pressures can be diffused when specialist staff are members of working parties established for planning and implementing equal opportunity policies, or for raising race equality issues. Such groups vary in their terms of reference, their membership and their status in the organisation, but their roles frequently include information-collection about what is currently happening in the organisation and about methods of implementing change which are under consideration or in operation elsewhere.

Opening up the organisation

In some voluntary organisations, 'opening up the organisation' is not seen as an issue. As services, local groups and jobs exist, it is expected that individual black people will take the opportunities thus presented. When such complacency is dented, and there is recognition that there may be barriers of many kinds preventing equal access, or equal treatment when access problems are overcome, organisations tackle the matter in a variety of ways. What they do may be part of a programme to open up the organisation at all levels, or it may consist of one step seen as most urgent. Or what is done may be a matter of chance: in one organisation it was said that translated leaflets had arrived unsolicited, had seemed like a good thing, and had been distributed.

When national voluntary organisations go beyond lip service to equal opportunities in employment, and begin to look critically at their current practices, they sometimes find (as local authorities have done) that there is not one current personnel policy, but many, with a great many decision-makers. The issues then will be different in organisations of different sizes. Although the same principles may inform a policy for an organisation with 20 staff as for an organisation with 200 or 2000, the procedures adopted, and the priorities to be set, will necessarily be affected. Large organisations face issues about span of effective control; small organisations face issues about the maintenance of flexibility, and a realistic approach to changing the composition of the workforce when turnover is low. Organisations concerned with disability sometimes find difficulty in balancing their responsibilities to people with the particular disability and their wider aims of being good 'all-around' equal opportunity employers. In one case, recognition of what it really meant to be an equal opportunity employer led the director to remove the statement about being an equal opportunity employer from his organisation's job advertisements; he hoped that as further progress was made they would be justified in reinserting it.

Much guidance is available about equal opportunity employment policies and practices, although organisations have had to find their own pattern related to their own circumstances, often through widespread consultation within the organisation. Less guidance is available 'off the peg' about ways of opening up other aspects of the organisation. In any case, these have to be related closely to the aims of the organisation, how it is structured, whether it provides services (and if so whether through written material, branches, social work visits or by telephone), if it is a self-help organisation, and so on.

One obvious step when new projects are to be started, or staff to be deployed or redeployed, is to choose locations where black populations are known to be concentrated. More difficult is the opening up of existing projects or groups. In one organisation, development staff arranged for black social workers from the social services department to attend a local group meeting in order to explain to existing white members what the experience and possible needs of local black families might be. Within the NDCS, an Asian mothers' group has been established as part of the Bradford branch.[5]

Perhaps the most common step taken in attempting to open up voluntary organisations is to provide translated materials. The translations can be of many kinds and serve many purposes. They may explain an organisation's role; the nature of the disability; welfare benefits; opening hours and services of local clinics and other sources of support and advice. In the case of Contact a Family's Southall project, the development worker spoke of translating CaF's local branch newsletter (which previously Asian fathers, but few Asian mothers, had been able to read) and of translating notes from the local special schools about coffee mornings and other opportunities for parents to be involved. In the Spastics Society's Kirklees project (funded under the Community Programme), translation was considered so important that one of the posts in the team was designated especially for this, although the postholder also acted as an interpreter for visitors to the office; in addition to translating information about the Society, the possibility of translating professional materials had been actively pursued.

Translations can be of existing material, or they can be written from scratch to cover the same ground more effectively; they can be provided on one side of a sheet of paper or take the form of substantial booklets; they can be carefully drafted to take into account differing concepts of health and disability, or they can be superficial and misleading. One director noted that when he first came to the organisation he discovered an information booklet available in seven minority languages as well as English. The one in English was 'nicely produced' but the others were duplicated and tatty. What was worse was that while the original English version had been withdrawn as no longer adequate, the translated versions were still distributed because demand from service-providers persisted in the absence of other relevant material. Eventually a complaint about the offensiveness of one translation led to the withdrawal of all the booklets.

Where voluntary organisations make substantial use of volunteers they sometimes recognise the need to take specific steps if they are to recruit (and retain) black volunteers. The fullest published account of an attempt to open up an organisation in this way is the report of the 1980-82 Kirklees Citizens Advice Bureau ethnic minorities advice project,[6] but increasing interest in the subject has led to a pilot survey on *Black People and Volunteering*,[7] carried out among 162 people in London in 1987 by the Black Perspectives in Volunteering Group and ADVANCE.

Even when organisations begin to have more black members, or more black staff, management or advisory groups may remain all white. Sometimes change comes naturally, as black people come into such roles through the ordinary processes of the organisation, but in other cases the importance of including a black voice in such bodies may seem too urgent to wait for this, and someone is brought in from outside. In one organisation, there was reported to be disappointment that a black person who had been invited to join an advisory group was not a regular attender, and that in any case he seemed unwilling to give the organisation either the lead – or the sharp prod – it needed; there was no suggestion that his own view of the matter had been sought. Even when there is recognition of the possible difficulties, for the organisation and the individual, when a single appointment of this kind is made, organisations sometimes seem to feel they have no alternative.

One of the ways used to open up voluntary organisations is by changing their public face: ensuring that black people are included in photographs in annual reports or leaflets or in television 'charity slots'; and ensuring that the way in which the organisation is presented in job advertisements or in offices gives black people confidence that it will be worthwhile to apply for jobs, services or membership. As organisations become more multiracial, with black staff and volunteers as well as members and service users, their public face naturally reflects this, but sometimes photographs and text seem to be used as token gestures rather than relating to the reality of experience in the organisation. With the heightened profile of race equality issues in the voluntary sector and in society as a whole, organisations have become more conscious of their image in this respect; whether a multiracial image is or is not presented in particular circumstances is perhaps now more likely to be a deliberate decision than a matter of chance.[8]

One of the factors in the decision is likely to be the expected effect on funders. There may be a conflict between reassuring local and central government that responsibilities to a multiracial public are being taken seriously, and anxiety about possible adverse effects on fundraising through individual donations and legacies. However, some organisations deliberately highlight race equality aspects of their work: NDCS headquarters used National Deaf Children's Week during 1986 to bring to public attention some of the professional and practical issues involved.

Increasing awareness in the organisation

One of the most difficult tasks for many voluntary agencies moving towards race equality is to find the right balance and timing between opening up the organisation, and raising awareness and expertise in the organisation. Most obviously, there seems little point in providing translated material which encourages people who speak English slightly or not at all to seek advice or support from an organisation if no arrangements have been made to ensure that there are staff available who speak their language or are equipped to deal with the matter through obtaining interpreters or in other ways. Similarly, there can be major problems in appointing a single black member of staff to fulfil an advisory role, without previously ensuring that existing staff are prepared to accept such a role and to consider seriously any issues raised, and that managers are equipped to deal responsibly with racism if it surfaces.[9]

On the other hand, when the importance of increasing awareness in the organisation is recognised, and many resources put into this, the difficulties which sometimes arise and the consequent energy and resources pre-empted can mean that sight is lost (at least temporarily) of the intended aim of opening up the organisation. Increasing the awareness of individuals becomes an end in itself, rather than a step towards change of other kinds.

Training seems to be recognised throughout the voluntary sector as having an important role to play in raising awareness and increasing skills. The type of training which is most appropriate and effective is still a matter of some dispute, not least because of the need to find a balance between change in the individual and change in the organisation. However, the trend has been away from racism awareness or anti-racist training brought in as a package, and towards training (whether by in-house or external trainers) which raises awareness within the context of the organisation's own setting and development.

In one small national organisation, outside trainers were chosen with considerable care as 'the people who do your training are crucial', and planning for the training took place over a period of five months to ensure the most effective format and the least disruption to the work of the organisation. A fortnight afterwards the trainers returned for discussion of the course, and further follow-up was planned. All staff and some of the voluntary members of the management committee participated in the training, and a number of individual and organisational initiatives were set in train. The director summed up the experience by saying enthusiastically that the training had been 'the big thing that has made all the difference'.

Another example of careful planning for a training event is Barnardo's London Division 'Issues of Race Conference'. At least one conference a year is organised for the Division on a subject of current professional importance, and the opportunity was taken in 1987 of focussing on race. The objectives were 'to take stock of the present situation in the Division' and 'to plan to put anti-racist initiatives into practice and monitor what we do'. The training was planned over many months, and included workshops addressed to practical issues within the Barnardo context. The resulting recommendations were being used in planning new initiatives by the Divisional Management Team (for whom there had already been a two-day training course in 1985).[10]

As an addition or alternative to training, some voluntary organisations have employed consultants to work with staff on an occasional or regular basis, helping them recognise issues and deal with them effectively within the specific organisational context. The Home Office's Voluntary Services Unit made funds available to NCVO for a three-year project (1985-88) to develop such work, which took the form of a variety of one-off and continuing projects. The organisations benefiting from this funding were expected to share their learning through regular participation in a group called VOSEM (Voluntary Organisations Services to Ethnic Minorities).

Although specific training or consultation initiatives can prove invaluable in beginning to raise awareness and shift attitudes, or to consolidate skills, both in social services departments and in voluntary organisations it is the availability of advice or support on an informal, continuing basis which can make a critical difference. A number of organisations which were lucky enough, or skilled enough, to make appointments (even when isolated ones) of especially talented black workers were benefiting in many ways from the questions raised by such staff; the example they gave of different ways of working; their ability to point to 'the normality of difference'; their sensitivity to racism, inadvertent discrimination and institutional racism and their openness in discussing these. One such worker described a critical aspect of her role as saying to statutory service-providers: 'Please listen: these things are important' – but that seems just as necessary within voluntary organisations.

Some of the methods which aim to collect information or to open up the organisation are also likely to raise awareness in the organisation. The 'position statement' which social services departments often prepare as an early step in any race equality initiative invariably serves this purpose, as it is commonly found that many members of staff have never previously considered the relevance of race equality to their part of the department's work. Such initial reviews seem less frequent in the voluntary sector, although the questionnaire which organisations completed in 1983 for the NCVO's working party clearly filled something of the same role in some cases.[11] As part of the preparation for Barnardo's London Division 1987 conference, mentioned above, all projects were asked to respond to a survey about their methods and success in recruitment of black staff, training events attended, numbers of black children and families involved in the project, 'initiatives to introduce white children to racism awareness', and other subjects. Since 1982 the projects had been asked to include in their annual reports for the Division's planning process information about how they were tackling race issues. Although such requests for information sometimes elicit only superficial responses, they can push previously unaware or uncertain staff into focussing their attention on specific components of change.

Many organisations have working parties on race equality or more general equal opportunities issues. Sometimes these are ad hoc staff interest or 'ginger' groups, whose role is to raise issues and awareness within the organisation; sometimes they are established to carry out detailed preparation of equal opportunities programmes, and then to follow through their implementation. In either case, there is always the danger that the group will be seen (and sometimes resented) as something apart from the 'ordinary' work of the organisation, and will have a decreasing role in raising awareness as implementation of change proves slow and initial enthusiasm wanes. Where organisations are aware of these dangers they use a variety of methods to diminish them – through ensuring members are drawn from across the organisation, by arranging that there will be a standing agenda item on the subject in decision-making committees, through involvement in training and in other ways. A few voluntary organisations have, however, already reached the stage where awareness of race equality issues is widespread, and race equality has become part of mainstream thinking and planning within the organisation; in such cases race equality working parties may wither away, or become part of groups working towards wider equal opportunity objectives.

Although 'raising awareness in the organisation' has been discussed third rather than first in this chapter, most discussions of change towards race equality in the voluntary sector are permeated by this issue throughout. One of the major challenges which organisations face is finding ways of using any changes implemented (whether piecemeal, precarious or planned) to increase awareness as widely as possible, and to increase it in a constructive fashion so that it is not free-floating but its connections with the ethos and work of the organisation are clear. That requires a systematic approach to change, whatever the content of change, and in the next chapter some relevant questions are suggested.

Notes

1 Some idea of the kinds of helpful detail which might be available can be seen in Jean Ellis' three anonymised case studies in 'Management committees and race equality' (NCVO *MDU Bulletin*, no.5, June 1985); in her account of community development with Asian communities (*Breaking New Ground*, Bedford Square Press, 1989); and in Priscilla Annamanthodo's fictionalised case study of a CVS in *Racism in Britain* (CVS-NA, 1987, pp.65-68). Nigel Harvey has described in detail both the problems and the successes in

establishing (together with the National Eczema Society) a group for Bangladeshi parents of children with eczema: 'Starting where the client is: some first steps towards making health care more accessible to ethnic minority users' (*Practice*, vol.2 no.2, 1988, pp.130-138). Much of the experience of social services departments is relevant to the voluntary sector: the most detailed account of change written from inside a department is Barney Rooney's *Racism and Resistance to Change: A study of the Black Social Workers Project*, Liverpool Social Services Department (University of Liverpool Department of Sociology, Merseyside Area Profile Group, 1987).

2   Christina Lee and Barry Howe, *Newham Way: Residents' views of the London Borough of Newham*, Barnardo's London Division, 1984.

3   Alys Woolley and Balwinder Dhanoa, *A Study of Asian Families with Handicapped Children in Smethwick*, ICAA West Midlands Regional Office, 1985. (Invalid Children's Aid Association – ICAA – has changed its name to Invalid Children's Aid Nationwide – I CAN.)

4   Jane Speedy, 'Ethnic minorities initiative', *Talk*, no.118, Winter 1985, p.12; and see the other articles in the issue's 'special report on deaf children and ethnic minorities in Britain today'.

5   Simon O'Hagan, 'A challenge that can be overcome', *Talk*, no.118, Winter 1985, p.16.

6   Dave Brunwin and Ray Cowell, *Kirklees Ethnic Minorities Advice Project: Final report*, National Association of Citizens Advice Bureaux, CAB Occasional Paper 16, 1984.

7   Hedley Taylor, *Black People and Volunteering*, ADVANCE, 1988.

8   The public face of disability organisations is a matter of considerable current controversy, with pressure mounting for organisations to abandon advertising campaigns which portray people with disabilities as helpless, and as 'natural' recipients of charity: Susan Scott-Parker, *They Aren't in the Brief*, King's Fund, 1989.

9   One of the black workers interviewed by Melba Wilson ('One black face', *New Society*, 19/26 December 1986 – Voluntary Action insert p.iii) said that being the single black person in an otherwise all-white voluntary organisation led 'to burn-out, feelings of exposure without support, and racist harassment, in the sense of being marginalised and ignored'.

10 Barnardo's London Division, *A Report for Participants in the Divisional Conference about Issues of Race – 20.2.87*.

11 The questionnaire is reproduced on pp.45-46 of Michaela Dungate, *A Multi-Racial Society: The role of national voluntary organisations*, NCVO, 1984.

4   Issues for organisations

The previous chapters have outlined the many ways in which voluntary organisations approach the question of their roles and responsibilities in a multiracial society, and the kinds of steps which they are taking. Consideration of the range of views, the types of activity and the variety of methods used provokes a number of questions which are sometimes explicitly voiced within voluntary organisations, but which more frequently seem implicit. These questions are:

1. What is it appropriate for us, as the kind of organisation we are, to do?
2. What resources are required, and are these available inside or outside the organisation?
3. What should be the scope and content of change?
4. How can implementation begin and proceed?
5. How can we maximise the effectiveness of change?

It has to be recognised that, as one informant put it, 'asking questions has a cost'. However, given the necessity of complying with the Race Relations Act 1976 by ensuring that neither direct nor indirect discrimination is taking place, and given the ethos of service of the voluntary sector, to raise such questions specifically, and make a serious attempt to answer them, seems a minimum obligation for any national voluntary organisation. In this chapter, the five questions are addressed, drawing on some aspects of the experience of organisations at various stages of development of race equality policies and practices.

1. What is it appropriate for us, as the kind of organisation we are, to do?

This is the basic question, and in a sense all organisations demonstrate their answers to it in the activities which they undertake. Once asked explicitly, its complexities become obvious. Of relevance are the size, structure, history, ethos and financial sources and circumstances of the organisation; its stated aims and the methods currently used to achieve them; the attitudes and awareness of staff and others involved in the organisation; the changes which have already taken place in an ad hoc or incremental fashion; and others. A first step is critical review of current operations, followed by re-examination of aims and methods and of the organisation's capacity for change; in all these, drawing on the views and experience of people in black organisations or within black communities is crucial.

1.1 *Critical review.* Depending on the type and scale of operations of the organisation, critical review can be a relatively simple or a very demanding process. However, it is hard to see how organisations can be certain that they are complying with their statutory obligations under the Race Relations Act 1976 without some such review. In any case, the idea of critical review may be more accepted now than formerly, given the many challenges faced by national voluntary organisations – moving away from residential provision, responding to pressures for involvement of service users, the prospects of taking on greater responsibilities for service provision following the 1988 Griffiths' report[1] and the 1989 community care White Paper,[2] and others. All these have pushed some traditional voluntary organisations into self- questioning and then review, and converted the continuous self-questioning of some other organisations into more systematic review. Inclusion of race equality dimensions as part of such reviews is important, but most organisations will still require specific review of how the organisation is responding to the needs of diverse communities and the circumstances of a multiracial society.

1.2 *Re-examination of aims and methods.* Once organisations begin to look systematically at what they are currently doing and why, across all aspects of their work in a multiracial, multicultural, multilingual society, questions arise not just about how adequately they are now meeting their stated aims, but whether the aims themselves need rethinking. In many cases the aims may well withstand scrutiny from new perspectives involving race equality and equal opportunities but in others they may not.

Aims, structures, membership criteria, methods of providing information and support, location of projects, and many other aspects of the functioning of an organisation may require fresh consideration in light of information about changing populations, locally or nationally: the extent and nature of diversity, demographic factors, special needs or extreme deprivation, prevalence of discrimination and racism, incidence of particular disabilities or illnesses and combinations of these, and so on. Methods of work may require modification, too, in light of changing policies and practices of complementary or overlappping providers, changing views of professionalism and obligations to funders. Founders' intentions and charity registration requirements may set the parameters of possible change, but within those parameters there will be decisions to be made about appropriate and feasible directions.

As well as reconsideration of the general aims of the organisation, specific aims in relation to race equality or equal opportunities may need consideration and clarification. Problems can arise once organisations move beyond paying lip service to such concepts, and attempt to put them into operation. In local authorities a particular issue has been the emphasis to be placed on equal access, in relation to that on equal outcomes; when such differences have not been sorted out at an early stage effective implementation of policy has in some cases been adversely affected. In the voluntary sector, where discussion is often in terms of anti-racism, it may be important to clarify whether that is indeed the aim – the objective towards which the organisation is working – or whether anti-racism is, rather, a necessary but not sufficient aspect of moving towards the more positive aim of race equality. Requiring clarification, too, is how work directed towards race equality will relate to other aspects of equal opportunities, and how priorities will be decided.

1.3 *Capacity for change.* The way in which national voluntary organisations are structured affects the capacity for implementing change. In one national organisation, for example, a senior officer referred to 'a mass of autonomous regions', while in another the regions were said to be 'like different countries'. In some organisations, local groups are independent bodies only loosely attached to the centre; in others, the organisation has a strong ethos of member decision-making at all levels. The capacity to introduce change (whether from the bottom or the top) will be affected by all these.

But it is not just the structure of organisations and relationships between different parts of them which affect capacity for change. Consultants and others attempting to advise on or implement change in the direction of race equality in voluntary organisations regularly report their despair at finding that a major impediment to change is administrative and organisational confusion – or apparent chaos. Even relatively straightforward changes can founder because of a lack of infrastructure for introducing change of any kind in a systematic manner.[3] On the other hand, as one development officer put it, 'If you have good management you can move ahead, not fall apart, not get stuck with all these contradictions and issues.' Thus, considering what it is appropriate for the organisation to do in relation to race equality may point to other kinds of changes which must be set in train at the same time.

1.4 *Relationships with people from black organisations and black communities.* Critical review and re-examination of aims and methods need to draw on the experiences and views of black people, if there is to be any realistic assessment of the current position, the need and capacity for change, and the forms this might take. At the same time, some preliminary consideration of the relevant issues is probably necessary at senior levels within the organisation before asking for help from people outside: with the availability now of much published material about ideas and experience in both voluntary and statutory sectors, it should be possible to begin the dialogue from a basis which is not so naive, patronising or guilt-ridden as has sometimes been reported (or self-reported) in the past.

A difficult and often contentious area is what the organisation's role should be (nationally or locally) in relation to black groups with overlapping interests. As noted in chapter one, issues about such relationships should be on the review agenda – the existence of black organisations attempting to meet the same or similar needs is not a reason for abdicating responsibility for review. Maureen Stone has argued that the traditional voluntary sector:

still claims to serve 'the community' including people from a minority background ... This means that the TVS [traditional voluntary sector] sees itself as entitled to funds to improve its services to minority communities, and it does not see this as competing with or threatening the BVS [black voluntary sector] in any way. In this scheme of things the BVS is seen as complementing, through the provision of specialist services, the general work of the TVS.

She goes on to comment caustically that this is not a view which wins wide support in the black voluntary sector.[4]

2. What resources are required, and are these available inside or outside the organisation?

In many voluntary organisations, pursuing a race equality programme or even taking a single step is only considered if extra resources are known to be readily available. In others, the issues are seen as important enough, and relevant enough for the organisation, to warrant drawing on existing budgets or actively seeking additional sources of funds. Even when financial resources are obtainable, other resources are required: those of expertise, and those of time.

2.1 *Financial resources.* The availability of financial resources is necessarily among the first questions which organisations raise when considering new policies or projects. Even when organisations have an annual turnover of millions of pounds, they sometimes argue that every penny is already fully committed and there is nothing to spare for work on race equality. Yet other organisations, working on a much smaller scale, find it possible to designate part of existing training or other budgets for race equality work. In one small national organisation, a special fund was initially established, but with the understanding that each section of the organisation would subsequently find the necessary funds to continue the work from mainstream allocations.

In many organisations, staff undertaking new work are themselves expected to find additional resources for this. One regional officer, for example, made plain that only her salary and some administrative assistance would be forthcoming from headquarters; her remit was to establish new projects through a mixture of local authority, central government and possibly other funding. There are clearly advantages in this requirement: to the organisation, which increases its resources and raises its profile; to the officers involved, who may have considerable freedom in planning activities without the necessity of arguing with colleagues over priorities for use of a central budget. New projects get off the ground, as external funding is usually easier to obtain for such projects than for core functioning or incremental change in existing work. But there are difficulties, too – many of which have been described by Bill Jordan in *The Use of the Community Programme in Health and Social Care*[5] – and such difficulties may be particularly marked (for the organisation as well as intended service users) if time-limited, precarious funding of a variety of kinds is drawn on in an attempt to meet needs of black communities.

During recent years, social services departments have begun to make much greater use of Section 11 funding from the Home Office to pay salaries of staff in specialist social work and other posts, and regret is often expressed by voluntary organisations that this is not available to them.[6] The regret is sometimes coupled with assurances that if Section 11 had been available they would long since have embarked on change. In the absence of this resource one organisation had applied to the Greater London Council for funding for an advisory race equality post, but the application was withdrawn when it was realised that abolition of the GLC meant that such money would have been available for only a brief period. Another organisation had applied for DHSS Section 64[7] funding for posts to investigate the need for its services among a number of specific ethnic minority communities; there had been long delay in obtaining a response and the organisation had taken no further steps while waiting.

Sometimes external funding is available specifically for race equality work; sometimes it is easier to make a case for project funding when the project is concerned with meeting needs of black communities, because it is so clearly new work for the organisation. But in considering the availability of resources of any kind for the organisation – whether continuing or new core funding, or funding for new work – funders increasingly have themselves been raising questions about how adequately organisations have responded to the multiracial nature of the local area or of Britain more generally. Local authorities which have introduced equal opportunities policies have been concerned that the voluntary organisations which they fund should function in accordance with the same principles. Sometimes a minimal compliance is all that is required, but in other cases a much more proactive stance is expected (the GLC's guidelines referred to organisations working 'actively in support' of the Council's anti-racist objectives). The Home Office Voluntary Services Unit in 1986 prepared a guidance note on race issues for central government departments funding voluntary organisations; according to the introduction

> Government is committed to a racially fair and just society in which black people have a sense of belonging. It has declared its unqualified opposition to racial discrimination, and seeks to promote equality of opportunity throughout society. Officials responsible for administering Government grants to voluntary organisations therefore have a duty to promote this policy among those receiving grants.[8]

2.2 *Expertise.* The issues about resources are not just issues about money, but also about expertise. Sometimes organisations which are committed to re-examining their aims and work in light of race equality objectives have sufficient in-house experience to do so, but in others they feel the need for some guidance, as well as the more critical examination of current functioning which someone can bring from outside. The consultancies arranged through NCVO, and the Anti-Racism Consortium project begun among a number of voluntary organisations in 1986, were intended to fill this need. Considerable preliminary work is probably required in-house, however, if consultants are to be accepted and consultancies are to prove effective.[9] Where the expertise is sought through advertising for experienced, senior black staff, national voluntary organisations frequently report difficulties in attracting applicants; having recognised the need for such expertise, some organisations then react to lack of applicants by shelving planned work, while others redouble their efforts to recruit appropriate people.

2.3 *Time.* Often overlooked in considering the resources necessary to consider race equality issues effectively is time, but this is invariably mentioned by all organisations which have made serious attempts to determine and implement race equality policies and programmes. Time is needed for review, the search for financial resources or for rejigging budgets, ascertaining appropriate changes, and many other aspects of new policies and practices. In addition, few other suggested changes arouse such intense feelings, or such a need to talk things through if perceptions are to shift and existing skills to be built on effectively.

3. *What should be the scope and content of change?*

Once organisations begin to ask questions in a systematic way about what they are doing and why, and what they might do additionally, they are faced with questions about the scope and content of change which hardly surfaced previously. The question of the scope of change – which aspects of the organisation to tackle, which to tackle first, and how many to tackle at once – is inevitably a difficult one. Questions of content can be equally difficult: once an area of change is decided on, just what should be done differently? Sometimes the answer is obvious; in other cases it is less so. Among the many decisions to be made in considering scope and content are relationships to statutory provision, whether change should be in the mainstream of the organisation's work or through special projects, and what priorities should be.

3.1 *Relationship to statutory provision.* This relationship is almost always a sensitive one for voluntary organisations, and can be particularly so when the issues are those of information, advice, support and care for people in black communities. When a voluntary organisation institutes work in this area, is it relieving a statutory agency of responsibility which the latter should be accepting? Will it be possible to demonstrate professionalism, without being seen as encroaching on statutory professionals' territory? Will the service provided by the voluntary organisation be less adequate than that provided to others by the statutory body through its mainstream work, so black people are in effect getting a second-class service? Will the voluntary service be precarious, so that aims have to be short-term rather than planned to encourage spin-offs and increase self-help?

Sometimes the needs tackled by a particular project seem so urgent and dire – for example, the situation of some Asian families with a number of severely handicapped children – that anything that can be done seems better than nothing. In any case, Asian staff of voluntary organisations making initial contact with such families often describe them as having given up hope of reaching any understanding or real communication with staff of statutory agencies (not least because of turnover of staff).[10] In these circumstances some voluntary organisations try to meet immediate needs as adequately as possible and stop there. Others use the information and contacts gained to inform and encourage statutory agencies through informal or formal training of practitioners, or participation in policy or planning groups. Thus, for example, Contact a Family's Southall worker was asked to join the governing bodies of local special schools. NDCS's Education Officer ensured that information about the Society's 'ethnic minorities initiative' was included in her regular talks at training colleges for teachers of deaf people; she also joined with the Open University to organise workshops at which such teachers could meet black parents.

3.2 *Mainstream vs. special.* Another major area of decision-making for voluntary organisations is whether to institute change in the mainstream of its work, or whether to establish special projects to meet needs seen as specific to certain groups in the black population – and if so whether these should be seen as short-term measures with subsequent absorption into the mainstream. Voluntary organisations beginning to consider the scope and content of change often seem to start from the assumption that special projects are required. Leaving aside the question of resource availability, this may in some circumstances be the best way forward given the difficulty of changing how existing staff or groups function, the need to concentrate expertise, or uncertainty about the viability of new methods. But special projects can easily be marginalised or compartmentalised, while the rest of the organisation goes on as before. On the other hand, if the emphasis is on mainstream change, progress may be too slow to be visible to most people within the organisation – or to be of value to black people requiring the kind of support or help which is intended.[11]

3.3 *Prioritising.* In determining the scope and content of change, many decisions arise about priorities: what should be tackled first, how proactive to be, and the amount of effort to be devoted to what is done in relation to other work or issues. One director summed up his organisation's current approach to race equality work as 'not ignoring it but not concentrating on it' – but some specific concentration is necessary if the steps taken are not to be merely tokens. A frequent difficulty, in local authorities as in voluntary organisations, has been that so much effort is put into necessary inputs that sight is lost – at least temporarily – of the desired outcomes. 'Solutions' are found for short-term problems without working towards answers which might be more satisfactory in the longer term. Thus one project might spend considerable time taking children to hospital appointments or school, while another, at the same time as helping mothers of disabled children in this way, makes application to the Family Fund for driving lessons for the mothers.

This is an example of what is, of course, a familiar quandary in the voluntary sector: is the aim to help people, or to give them the support to help themselves? But it arises with particular force when the people seeming to need help have little command of English, and are living in extremely stressful and/or isolated conditions. Another familiar quandary, and one which needs careful consideration when race equality work is being planned, is how to keep the appropriate balance between meeting the needs of volunteers or those on training schemes (whether black or white) and those of black service recipients.

4. *How can implementation begin and proceed?*

Questions of implementation arise as soon as organisations move beyond ad hoc, piecemeal change. One of the clearest lessons of local authority experience over the past decade is that what is decided at policy levels may end there, may never be reflected in day-to-day functioning unless attention is paid to details of implementation. Merely telling staff to get on with implementation is insufficient. The same is true in voluntary organisations, and among the questions which have to be tackled is whether special posts or arrangements will be required for implementation, how the work of various parts of the organisation can most effectively be meshed, and whether management will require new skills.

4.1 *Special arrangements*. One of the most common arrangements made in order to get race equality policy implementation under way is the establishment of a working party. Sometimes these grow out of ad hoc staff interest groups, which are given responsibility for considering the form and implementation of change once the organisation decides to take on race issues in a more systematic way. Working party remits may be solely about race equality issues, or they may extend to equal opportunities in relation also to gender, disability and sexual orientation. The emphasis is often initially on recruitment, selection and other aspects of equal opportunity employment policies, but all aspects of the work of the organisation may be within the terms of reference.

Composition of such groups varies, depending in part on the job they are expected to do: participants may be self-chosen from among those most committed to change, or they can represent the various sections of the organisation. Sometimes only paid staff are involved; sometimes voluntary workers or voluntary members of management committees participate. In one organisation, outsiders with special expertise to contribute were also invited to attend: from the Commission for Racial Equality, a central government department and a disability umbrella group. Each way of organising race (or equal opportunities) working groups has pros and cons, but as noted earlier experience in local authorities suggests that when special arrangements of this kind are established, arrangements must also be made for ensuring there are specific ways for their deliberations and recommendations to work back into the ordinary processes of the organisation. That is, assuming that there is commitment to change in critical parts of the organisation: in discussing the reception of his working group's draft report, one director said sadly that he had learned a lot in recent months about 'the power of deliberate inertia'.

Organisations often also establish specialist posts as part of the implementation of race equality policies and practices. This can be seen in the organisation as part of its opening up through an equal opportunity employment programme, or it can be quite separate. The posts are sometimes concerned primarily with practice among users of the organisation's services, sometimes with developing the capacity of the organisation to respond more effectively in all aspects of its operations. Some idea of the kinds of contribution a specialist worker can make is given in a brief report on Barnardo's black project worker, appointed in 1985 to work with children and staff in seven Barnardo projects. Her post is said to require 'both commitment and sensitivity'; to this might be added understanding, flexibility – and great strength.[12]

Expectations of black people who fill such posts can be overwhelming. In some cases, appointments have been made with insufficient attention to the kind of experience required, or the necessary degree of matching of age, sex, religion and origins with those among whom development work is intended. In other cases, organisations have appointed someone of outstanding ability who has been able to develop the necessary support mechanisms to make the post practicable, when the organisation itself was not sufficiently experienced to prepare the ground in this way. In a few cases, however, senior staff who had been lucky enough to have such a staff member seemed reluctant to move ahead into further work, or work in other locations, until another exceptional person could be found.

4.2 *Meshing the organisation's work.* As noted earlier, few national voluntary organisations are likely to be starting from scratch when they begin to implement more systematic race equality policies and practices. In most cases, some changes at some points in the organisation will already have taken place in an ad hoc way. Some of the learning which has taken place will be about pitfalls, and what not to do again – 'disastrous' pilot projects are not unknown – but much of the experience gained can be of great advantage. In addition, staff who have come in from local authorities, or other voluntary organisations which have already embarked on systematic change towards race equality, may have ideas, enthusiasm and commitment. In any headquarters plans, therefore, ways have to be found of incorporating experience which may be located in far-flung parts of the organisation.

National voluntary organisations have, at least in theory, excellent opportunities for disseminating the results of work undertaken. More emphasis is placed on this in some organisations than in others. Among the examples given by those interviewed were regular meetings of regional officers at London headquarters, at which local project work with black communities was described; drawing on the experience of black staff in training courses and more informal learning occasions; and articles about current work and current issues in the organisation's journal. A regional development officer spoke of drawing on the experience of developing one project to establish another in a different city in a somewhat different way: dissemination came through the opportunities for him to pass on his own learning.

At an early stage in the development of one local authority's race equality policies, the chief executive pointed to progress already made in the social services department, and asked 'Do all the ships in the convoy have to go at the same speed?' Similar questions are often asked about national voluntary organisations, and in some cases adherence to the organisation's anti-racism or equal opportunities policy has become a condition of membership for local groups.

4.3 *Managing change.* The argument of consultants and others that a major impediment to introduction of race equality can be ineffective management and managerial structures raises the question of whether good management and sensible structures are sufficient. They may be necessary, but it is doubtful whether they are sufficient. Over and over again, in any research on implementation of race equality, white managers refer to the superficiality of their original understanding, and the way they have only gradually become fully aware of the issues and of the complexity of implementing change directed towards race equality. Significant degrees of commitment, of flexibility and determination are required, as well as knowledge going well beyond generalisations about cultural patterns or needs. Although these probably come largely through often-painful learning on the job, some organisations have recognised the need to give support and training to senior managers as an integral part of new developments. In one case, the director himself arranged to have supervision sessions with an outside race trainer as a way of continually testing out his ideas about progress within the organisation.

5. How can we maximise the effectiveness of change?

Voluntary organisations can answer this question at a number of different levels. 'Effectiveness' can be defined in terms of improving the public image of the organisation and encouraging funders to provide continuing or new support. Or it can be defined in relation to the success of internal arrangements for considering and progressing change: training courses welcomed, new recruitment and selection procedures introduced smoothly, and a growth of interest and awareness among paid and unpaid staff, voluntary members of management and other committees, and branch members.

Both these ways of looking at effectiveness are important, but clearly they can have drawbacks. Over-concern with public image can mean superficial change, with token gestures in line with current fashions. Over-concern with processes within the organisation can produce elegant solutions to the problems of organisational change, but ones which are self-contained and have little relationship to the actual effects for black people outside the existing organisation. Thus, in considering how to maximise effectiveness, concentration has to be focussed continually on what the outcomes of change are for people in black communities, whether they want to participate fully in the organisation, or need the advice, support or care offered.

The experience of the past decade, in both the statutory and voluntary sectors, points to ways of working which can at least help to maximise the effectiveness of change. These include provision of continuing encouragement and support to staff and others in grappling with new ideas and changed methods; and placing emphasis on increasing the capacity of all those in the organisation to recognise issues and respond to them rather than avoid them. In initial stages, some special projects may be necessary, and some special structures for implementing change, but these need to go along with mainstream change, and be linked as fully as possible with the ordinary arrangements of the organisation. Alertness to opportunities opening up is a necessary part of any strategy for change, but even if the steps taken have to be piecemeal or precarious, they can be taken within a general framework which allows the experience to be evaluated, disseminated, and used as the basis of further work.

In general, an evaluative approach to all change is necessary if organisations are to deal effectively with the complex questions which arise in implementation of race equality policies and practices. Such an approach must include ways of judging outcomes for black people. Numbers joining the organisation, or using its services, or working in paid or unpaid capacities, are of course important. Continuing critical evaluation, though, needs to take into account much more than numbers, and to look at the experience of black people in such involvement, and the relevance and quality of what they gain from it.

In introducing the case studies in *We want to be anti-racist but we don't know what to do* Christine Collins says:

> What emerges ... is that there is no blue-print which will be effective for all organisations, but that each organisation has to devise a strategy which is appropriate for its own structure, the service it provides and the people it is working for and with.[13]

Voluntary organisations which are only now beginning to move on from ad hoc change to a more strategic approach, or which are reconsidering their roles and responsibilities, can benefit from the wealth of experience in voluntary and statutory sectors during the 1980s. However, the ways in which such experience can be used will be affected by the many changes under way in the social care world: the next chapter draws attention to some of their implications.

Notes

1 Sir Roy Griffiths, *Community Care: Agenda for action*, HMSO, 1988.

2 Department of Health, *Caring for People: Community care in the next decade and beyond*, HMSO, Cm 849, 1989.

3 Examples of this can, of course, also be found in the statutory sector: see Linda Challis and others, *Review and Consolidation in Brent Social Services Department: Final report*, University of Bath Centre for the Analysis of Social Policy, 1987.

4 Maureen Stone, *Resourcing Black Voluntary Organisations: Funding for failure?*, Report to the Urban Unit, NCVO, 1986, p.13.

5 Bill Jordan, *The Use of the Community Programme in Health and Social Care*, NCVO, 1987.

6 Under Section 11 of the Local Government Act 1966 the Home Office is empowered to pay part of the salary costs of local authority staff employed 'in consequence of the presence within their areas of substantial numbers of immigrants from the Commonwealth whose language or customs differ from those of the community'. Following a 1988 efficiency scrutiny, new proposals for Section 11 were issued in March 1990. Greater access by voluntary organisations is a key part of these.

7 Section 64 of the Health Services and Public Health Act 1968 gives the Department of Health the power to make grants to voluntary organisations providing services similar to those provided by health and social services authorities.

8 Home Office Voluntary Services Unit, *Government-funded Organisations and Race: Guidelines*, 1986. An efficiency scrutiny of all central government funding of voluntary organisations was undertaken during 1989. No information is yet available as to whether race equality or equal opportunities will be part of any guidelines issued following the scrutiny.

9 For a frank history of the Anti-Racism Consortium, see Anne Sedley, *The Challenge of Anti-Racism: Lessons from a voluntary organisation*, Down's Syndrome Association, Family Service Units and Maternity Alliance, 1989.

10 Of course, statutory authorities themselves can retrieve the situation, rather than relying on voluntary organisations to do so. See, for example, the description of the Parent Advisory Scheme operated by the Tower Hamlets Child Development Team: Hilton Davis and Prapti Ali Choudhury, 'Helping Bangladeshi families', *Mental Handicap*, vol.16 (June 1988), pp.48-51.

11 In a recent initiative undertaken in the statutory sector, the Local Government Training Board and Focus Consultancy are working during 1989-90 with two

London social services departments specifically on 'bringing race and culture into the mainstream of social services provision'. The emphasis of the work in one department is on services to elderly Asian people and in the other on child protection in relation to the Afro-Caribbean community. The report of the work (publication is planned for September 1990) should provide information about the feasibility of mainstreaming of value to the voluntary sector as well as to social services departments. See 'Race and culture: new LGTB activities', p.8 of LGTB's *Training for Social Services*, no.13, September 1989.

12   Joan Fratter, 'Barnardo's black project worker', *Foster Care*, March 1986, p.15.

13   Christine Collins, *'We want to be anti-racist but we don't know what to do'*, London Voluntary Service Council, 1986.

5 Summary and conclusions

There were many significant changes in the voluntary sector in Britain during the 1980s. One of these changes was a greater awareness of and concern with issues of race equality as well as other aspects of equal opportunities. Although many national organisations are still reacting in an ad hoc fashion, others have attempted to tackle the issues in a more systematic way. In the process much has been learned, often through quite painful experience: it has been a challenging time.

Some national voluntary organisations show little recognition that the multiracial, multicultural, multilingual nature of British society has any significant implications for their roles and responsibilities. Such apathy is less likely now to take the form of a completely colourblind approach; instead, while it is accepted that something about the settings within which they work is different, a few token gestures are seen as a sufficient response. At the other extreme, some organisations are so overwhelmed by a sense of outrage at the position of black people in Britain today and the amount that therefore has to be done, and done by them, that they become deskilled and disabled. The position of most organisations is somewhere between such apathy and such outrage – but the range of possibilities is great.

There are many variations among organisations, but also within organisations. The awareness, attitudes and commitment of all those involved in the organisation are important in determining the extent to which it is opened up to black people, and whether policies and practices directed towards race equality can be raised and can be implemented. However, the role of senior staff is of especial importance: they can direct the attention of management and other committees to relevant issues, encourage initiatives throughout the

organisation and give continuing support to them, ensure
dissemination of ideas and experience, and forward systematic
attention to the subject in other ways. Yet many such staff show
considerable uncertainty about what they should and could be doing.

While recognising that issues of race equality exist (in itself a
significant advance from earlier positions), they may feel that no
special steps are necessary in their own organisation because the
professionalism of staff, or the kind of people they are, means that any
necessary changes will come naturally. Where an organisation has a
strong ethos of member decision- making senior staff may feel
inhibited from suggesting specific courses of action if members have
not raised the matter. Sometimes senior staff would like to institute
changes, but consider this impossible because of constrained
resources, or blockages at critical points.

On the other hand, aspects of the ethos of an organisation can
provide a spur to change; so too can pressure from within the
organisation from local groups, regional offices or members of
management committees. There is also increasingly likely to be
pressure for change from outside, from funders, umbrella
organisations, black organisations and others. The availability of
resources for training or for projects concerned with race equality or
services to local black communities provides another push towards
change.

That change takes many forms. It can be piecemeal, precarious or
planned. Indeed, at any one time organisations often show examples
of each of these. New policies and practices, and the scope and content
of change, are sometimes the subject of careful consideration, but
sometimes result from ad hoc responses to particular opportunities or
particular pressures, with no necessary connection between them, or
any attempt to disseminate the ideas and experience gained.

Much of the piecemeal or precarious work may be of great value,
both in developing the necessary awareness and expertise in some
parts of the organisation, and in providing opportunities or support for
some black people. But there also seems to be a substantial amount of
misconceived or misdirected effort, or effort which (while useful in
itself) is not utilised effectively. That may be because of insufficient
understanding of the situation, experience and needs of people in black
communities, or a superficial approach to change, or uncertainty about
the objectives of the work undertaken, or lack of capacity within the

organisation to make the necessary connections. However, even organisations which make a determined attempt to look systematically at their roles and responsibilities, and to plan a variety of changes across the work of the organisation, can face problems and setbacks. National voluntary organisations are complex – implementation of race equality policies and practices is also complex.

Organisations thus need as many sources of information and support as they can get if they are to avoid the pitfalls and move ahead more consistently and effectively. There is now a considerable amount of guidance published about how race equality and equal opportunities might be introduced in the voluntary sector; and there are many training and consultancy resources available. What is needed are detailed accounts of individual organisations' experience of change, making plain the problems but also how these are resolved; accounts of particular types of change in organisations of similar sizes and structures; and as far as possible information about what the outcomes have been. Information of this kind would be especially helpful to those organisations just beginning to ask themselves the kinds of basic questions suggested in chapter four of this paper.

In addition, such accounts are needed if we are to take stock, to judge just how far national voluntary organisations have come over the past decade. Clearly there is more awareness of race equality issues; clearly there is, in some organisations, a wholehearted commitment to considering what change might be appropriate and setting this in train. Yet it is impossible to make any overall assessment of the extent to which black people have access – routinely, and with confidence – to membership, to the opportunity to contribute in a voluntary or a paid capacity, or to the information, advice, advocacy, support or care which voluntary organisations are in the business of providing.

Many new challenges are now arising for all agencies concerned with social care. On the one hand, it is even more urgent that the experience of the 1980s should be as quickly and fully available as possible; on the other hand, the context in which it will be used will be markedly different following the community care White Paper, the National Health Service and Community Care Bill, and subsequent regulations and guidelines from the Department of Health. In addition, fuller implementation of the Disabled Persons (Services, Consultation and Representation) Act 1986 will have implications for many voluntary organisations.

Social services departments will be moving away from provision of care to encouraging the development of alternative providers, and contracting with them for specific sites or services (as, indeed, is already happening in many authorities). They will have new responsibilities for preparing community care plans for the locality, for assessment and for arranging packages of care. Many voluntary organisations are considering the contribution they can make in relation to these new responsibilities. They are also considering whether they should enter into contracts for provision of services, what terms would be appropriate and how other roles of the organisation (especially advocacy and campaigning) might be affected. Much work is being done on such issues by NCVO and others, and guidance notes on legal, ethical and practical aspects are appearing regularly.[1]

In this situation, some of the challenges facing national voluntary organisations in relation to race equality will be the same as they have been during the 1980s. They will need to find effective ways of opening up the organisation at all levels, and to find constructive working relationships with black organisations. There will be sensitive issues about whether all parts of the organisation proceed towards race equality in the same way and at the same speed. Ways of disseminating hard-won learning and experience throughout the organisation have to be found. There will be complex matters of implementing, managing and evaluating change. And there will be the critical importance of finding ways of judging outcomes.

The new context poses new issues, however, which make systematic review of race equality policies and practices even more urgent. As organisations try to come to grips with the new situation in the social care world they cannot put race equality aside: discussion of this has to be an integral part of decision-making about whether to bid for contracts, how continued receipt of grants will be justified, and what responsibility a national organisation has in contributing ideas, experience and principles to national guidelines.

At local levels, there will be a need to ensure that social services department community care plans take fully into account the implications of a multiracial society – and not just in terms of language and culture, but also showing a realistic appreciation of the constraints imposed by discrimination and by racial abuse, harassment and attack.

The same is true of representations made to the Department of Health and its Social Services Inspectorate, in relation to guidelines on managing a 'contract culture', and on training and assessment.

In deciding whether to bid for contracts, and in drawing up proposals for taking on tasks or services, existing issues about 'parachuting in' to localities arise with particular force. In considering the matter national organisations need to take account of the existence of local black groups, which may (to those awarding contracts) appear much less experienced, and possibly too great a risk.[2] How far do the responsibilities of the national organisation go in providing support and encouragement to such groups, or in suggesting forms of joint working?

When contract specifications are being drawn up, and the local authority's commitment to race equality and equal opportunities is clear, voluntary organisations will have to be able to give convincing evidence that they are competent to provide services effectively. Where there is less commitment or awareness, voluntary organisations can play a role in drawing the matter – and its detailed implications – to the attention of the contracting authority. In addition, in past discussions of the relative roles (and value) of statutory and voluntary provision of social care, the flexibility of the voluntary sector contribution has always been stressed. It will be especially important now for voluntary organisations, in discussion of contracts (or of grants with carefully-drawn conditions), to stress to local authorities the need to maintain as much flexibility as possible. This is necessary in any case if service users are to have an increasing voice in services, and if provision is to be individual-led rather than service-based; but all the experience of the past decade points to its especial importance in order to draw on increasing learning as work for and with black service users develops.

Finally, national voluntary organisations are in a position to take a broad view of developments over the coming years, as all these changes take effect. That places a particular responsibility on them to keep a watching brief on the way in which a contract culture and a multiplicity of providers of social care affect people in black communities. Neither apathy nor outrage can provide this: national voluntary organisations have to find somewhere in between these extremes which will make a contribution, and a substantial contribution, to progress towards race equality.

Notes

1 Christian Kunz, Rowan Jones and Ken Spencer, *Bidding for Change: Voluntary organisations and competitive tendering for local authority services following the Local Government Act 1988*, Birmingham Settlement Research Unit and Community Projects Foundation, 1989; Nick Fielding and Richard Gutch,*The Legal Context*, Guidance Notes on Contracting for Voluntary Groups No.1, NCVO, 1989; *The Contract Culture: The challenge for voluntary organisations*, Guidance Notes on Contracting for Voluntary Groups No.2, NCVO, 1989. The Guidance Notes are published by NCVO in conjunction with the Voluntary Sector Working Group on Contracting Out. In addition, NCVO's Community Care Project has issued a number of reports and briefing papers on contract issues.

2 See *How Do Contracts for Care Affect Black Groups?*, NCVO Community Care Project, 1989, and Arshi Ahmad, 'Contracting out of equal opportunities', *Social Work Today*, 19 October 1989, p.26.

References

Place of publication London unless indicated otherwise

Arshi Ahmad, 'Contracting out of equal opportunities', *Social Work Today*, 19 October 1989, p.26.

Coreen Allen and Judy Walker, *Implementing an Equal Opportunities Policy: A guideline for CVS*, Councils of Voluntary Service National Association, 1987.

Priscilla Annamanthodo, *Racism in Britain: Guidance for CVS and other local development agencies*, Councils of Voluntary Service National Association, 1987.

Barnardo's, *Racial Integration and Barnardo's: Report of a working party*, Barkingside, 1966.

Barnardo's London Division, *A Report for Participants in the Divisional Conference about Issues of Race – 20.2.87*, Barkingside, 1987.

Dave Brunwin and Ray Cowell, *Kirklees Ethnic Minorities Advice Project: Final report*, National Association of Citizens Advice Bureaux, CAB Occasional Paper 16, 1984.

Linda Challis and others, *Review and Consolidation in Brent Social Services Department: Final report*, University of Bath Centre for the Analysis of Social Policy, 1987.

Charity Commissioners for England and Wales, *The Promotion of Racial Harmony*, booklet CC17, 1989.

Juliet Cheetham, *Social Work Services for Ethnic Minorities in Britain and the U.S.A.: Final report of a study funded by the Department of Health and Social Security*, University of Oxford Department of Social and Administrative Studies, 1981.

Judith Citron, *Citizens Advice Bureaux: For the community, by the community*, Pluto Press, 1989.

Christine Collins, '*We want to be anti-racist but we don't know what to do*', London Voluntary Service Council, 1986.

Naomi Connelly, *Race and Change in Social Services Departments*, Policy Studies Institute, Discussion Paper 27, 1989.

Hilton Davis and Prapti Ali Choudhury, 'Helping Bangladeshi families', *Mental Handicap*, vol.16, June 1988, pp.48-51.

Paul Davison, *Ideas into Action: Notes produced by a BASSAC members' workshop*, British Association of Settlements and Social Action Centres, 1986.

Department of Health, *Caring for People: Community care in the next decade and beyond*, HMSO, Cm 849, 1989.

Sheena Dunbar and Laurence Ward, *A Guide to the Implementation of an Equal Opportunity Policy*, MIND South East, 1987.

Michaela Dungate, *A Multi-Racial Society: The role of national voluntary organisations* (Report of the Ethnic Minorities Working Party), National Council for Voluntary Organisations, 1984.

Jean Ellis, 'Management committees and race equality: anti-racism in the voluntary sector – a picture of inaction', Supplement to NCVO *MDU [Management Development Unit] Bulletin*, no.5, June 1985.

Jean Ellis, *Breaking New Ground*, Bedford Square Press, 1989.

Nick Fielding and Richard Gutch, *The Legal Context*, Guidance Notes on Contracting for Voluntary Groups No.1, NCVO, 1989.

Joan Fratter, 'Barnardo's black project worker', *Foster Care*, March 1986, p.15.

Sir Roy Griffiths, *Community Care: Agenda for action*, HMSO, 1988.

Nigel Harvey, 'Starting where the client is: some first steps towards making health care more accessible to ethnic minority users', *Practice*, vol.2 no.2, 1988, pp.130-138.

Home Office Voluntary Services Unit, *Government-funded Organisations and Race: Guidelines*, 1986.

Marc Jaffrey and Alan Farleigh, *Action not Words: Putting a race equality policy into practice*, Brighton Council for Voluntary Service, 1988.

Bill Jordan, *The Use of the Community Programme in Health and Social Care*, National Council for Voluntary Organisations, 1987.

Barry Knight and Anne Marie McDonald, *The Funding Relationship: Report of a conference on the funding of organisations managed by members of ethnic minorities*, Home Office Voluntary Services Unit, 1988.

Pradeep Kumar, *Ethnic Monitoring and VBX [volunteer bureaux]*, Berkhamsted, Volunteer Centre, 1986.

Christian Kunz, Rowan Jones and Ken Spencer, *Bidding for Change: Voluntary organisations and competitive tendering for local authority services following the Local Government Act 1988*, Birmingham Settlement Research Unit and Community Projects Foundation, 1989.

Christina Lee and Barry Howe, *Newham Way: Residents' views of the London Borough of Newham*, Barnardo's London Division, 1984.

Local Government Training Board, *Training for Social Services*, no.13, September 1989.

Lucy Macleod, *"Irrespective of race, colour or creed?": Voluntary organisations and minority ethnic groups in Scotland*, Edinburgh, Scottish Council for Voluntary Organisations, 1987.

NCVO, *The Contract Culture: The challenge for voluntary organisations*, Guidance Notes on Contracting for Voluntary Groups No.2, NCVO, 1989.

NCVO Community Care Project, *How Do Contracts for Care Affect Black Groups?*, 1989.

Simon O'Hagan, 'A challenge that can be overcome', *Talk* [National Deaf Children's Society], no.118, Winter 1985, p.16.

Kate Poulton, *Equal Opportunity Employment Policies: Guidelines for voluntary organisations*, North Kensington Law Centre Employment Rights Unit, 1986.

Jim Read, *The Equal Opportunities Book: A guide to employment practice in voluntary organisations and community groups*, InterChange Books, 1988.

Ann Richardson and Meg Goodman, *Self-Help and Social Care*, Policy Studies Institute, 1983.

Barney Rooney, *Racism and Resistance to Change: A study of the Black Social Workers Project, Liverpool Social Services*

Department, University of Liverpool Department of Sociology, . Merseyside Area Profile Group, 1987.

Pascoe Sawyers and Joy Fraser, *Bridges: A directory of African, Caribbean, Asian, Latin American and Mediterranean community groups in Greater London,* London Voluntary Service Council, 1988.

Susan Scott-Parker, *They Aren't in the Brief,* King's Fund, 1989.

Anne Sedley, *The Challenge of Anti-Racism: Lessons from a voluntary organisation,* Down's Syndrome Association, Family Service Units and Maternity Alliance, 1989.

Southwark Council for Voluntary Service, *Equal Opportunities: Some steps towards race equality in employment,* 1984.

Jane Speedy, 'Ethnic minorities initiative', *Talk* [National Deaf Children's Society], no.118, Winter 1985, p.12.

Maureen Stone, *Resourcing Black Voluntary Organisations: Funding for failure?,* Report to the NCVO Urban Unit, 1986.

Hedley Taylor, *Black People and Volunteering,* ADVANCE, 1988.

David N.Thomas, *White Bolts, Black Locks: Participation in the inner city,* Allen & Unwin, 1986.

Melba Wilson, 'One black face', *New Society,* 19/26 December 1986, Voluntary Action supplement p.iii.

Alys Woolley and Balwinder Dhanoa, *A Study of Asian Families with Handicapped Children in Smethwick,* ICAA West Midlands Regional Office, 1985.